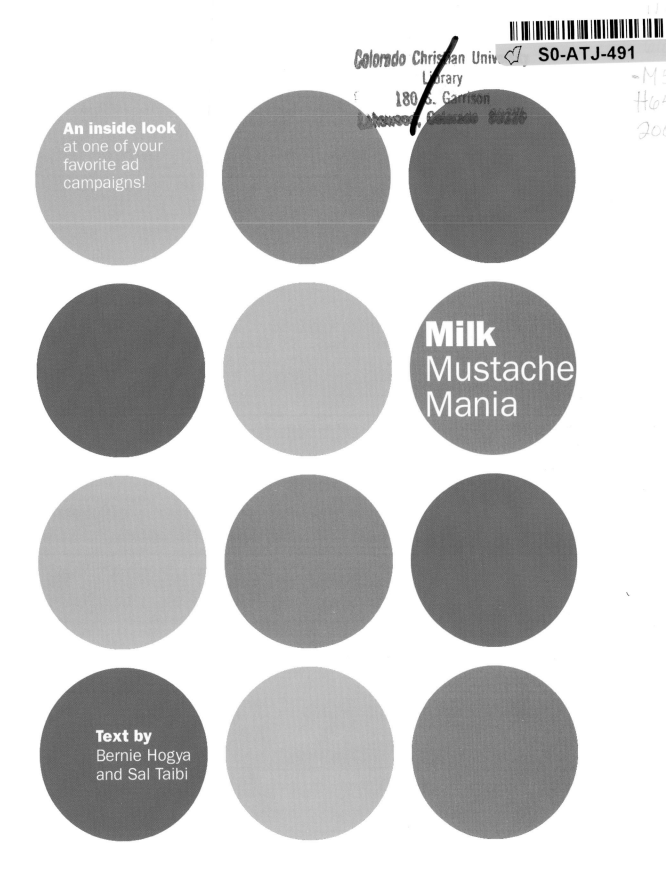

An inside look at one of your favorite ad campaigns!

Milk Mustache Mania

Text by Bernie Hogya and Sal Taibi

Scholastic Inc.

New York   Toronto   London   Auckland   Sydney

Mexico City   New Delhi   Hong Kong   Buenos Aires

ISBN 0-439-38889-9

12 11 10 9 8 7 6 5 4 3 2 1   1 2 3 4 5 6/0

Printed in the U.S.A.

First Scholastic printing, December 2001

Designed by Keirsten Geise

Contents

The Milk Mustache Campaign was launched in January of 1995. Since then it has been and continues to be one of the most popular advertising campaigns ever. We've found over the years that teenagers and kids like to collect the ads, hang them on their walls, trade them, and even sell them on eBay. If you're one of them, this book is for you.

Why Milk?

In the old days — before there were sports drinks, bottled iced tea, bottled water, diet soda, juice drinks, and calcium fortified juices — life was a lot simpler for milk. Today it is much tougher for milk to compete against so many beverage options.

These other products are fun to drink and, until recently, had more exciting advertising than milk. Yet milk is still pretty much one of the best things that you can drink. It's recommended by health and medical groups because it is such a great source of calcium. And every glass of milk contains nine essential nutrients that you need every day, no matter how old you are.

Why Teens?

You need to drink a lot of milk, but this is the time when you start drinking less of it. Why? Well, aren't you starting to get tired of doing what your parents and other people tell you to do?

When drinking milk is thought of as one of those things that you're told to do, instead of something you want to do, it's easy to give it up. Especially when there are so many other fun things to drink. But it's during your teen years that a "calcium crisis" begins to develop. When teens turn to other drinks — especially soft drinks that have no nutritional value — you start to become calcium deficient. This robs your bones of calcium when they need to grow and be strong. And if you don't get enough calcium now, there won't be anything that you can do about it when you get older. That's why we want you to know that milk is really important. It's not just for kids.

You're still growing — fifteen percent of your adult height is added during your teen years — and the nutrients in milk will help you to be better at work, play, and sports. It's funny how everyone starts out drinking a lot of it as a kid and then they seem to drink less and less as they get older. But people need to drink milk, no matter what their age. You should drink milk all through your life.

Why Kids?

One shift that has occurred with the Milk Mustache Campaign over the years has been to place more emphasis on ads for kids. Kids drink a lot of milk. But if you already drink a lot of it, why do we need to advertise to you? Well, you drink a lot of milk mostly because you are told to. Right? You're told by your mom, you're told by your school — you're always being told to "drink your milk." But we want you to have your own reasons to drink it. We want you to want to drink milk because it will help you grow, make you strong, help you play harder, and because it tastes good.

Why the Milk Mustache?

Our goal is to make sure that people of every age know that milk is important to drink. We also have to change the way that people think about milk. Plus, we want to give milk a contemporary image and keep it competitive in a very crowded beverage category. The Milk Mustache Campaign does all of these things. First, we show celebrities who drink milk. The people we feature are popular, healthy, and cool — the same qualities that we want milk to have. The "mustache" reminds people that milk tastes great and is fun to drink. Finally, the ad tells you all the great things about milk and why you should drink it.

Every month, a new milk mustache ad is launched. This helps keep the campaign fresh, surprising, and engaging. The reason that you don't ever seem to get tired of it is because there is always a new ad to look for — one that you've never seen before.

There is no doubt that the campaign has had an impact. It's changed the way people think about milk. It's made them think about milk. It's made milk cool. Milk has gone from being something that you have to drink to something you want to drink. In fact, more people remember seeing milk ads than they do ads for Coke and Pepsi. The campaign, along with dairy industry efforts like new packaging, new flavors, and new distribution channels, is helping to change the way that you drink milk.

Celebrities from television, sports, music, and movies jump at the chance to be in the Milk Mustache Campaign. The following pages showcase the latest ads and those celebrities that are proud to wear the milk mustache.

We hope that you'll join them.

Milk
Mustache
Mania

Television stars have always played a large role in the Milk Mustache Campaign. Stars from shows including Friends, Buffy the Vampire Slayer, *and* Dawson's Creek *as well as TV personalities like Conan O'Brien and Paul Shaffer appeared in the campaign's first years. The following are some of the popular TV personalities and shows that recently joined the campaign.*

Frasier **Cast**

We had always wanted to use the entire cast of a hit television show in a milk mustache ad, so when the producers of *Frasier* called, we jumped at the chance. In past ads we were limited to one or two stars from a show, like when we photographed Jimmy Smits and Dennis Franz from *NYPD Blue* or Jennifer Aniston and Lisa Kudrow from *Friends*.

This time it would be different.

Frasier was a top rated show when the cast agreed to be photographed for their milk mustache ad. The show had recently set an Emmy Awards record, becoming the first program to take top honors for an outstanding comedy series five years in a row.

We assembled the complete cast: Martin (John Mahoney) with Eddie, his lovable Jack Russell terrier (played by canine actor Moose), Bulldog (Dan Butler), Roz (Peri Gilpin), Frasier (Kelsey Grammer), Daphne (Jane Leeves), and Niles (David Hyde Pierce).

Not only was it the first ad to feature the entire cast of a show, it also set a record for the largest number of milk mustaches in one ad: six! And that number almost hit seven as Moose lunged out of John Mahoney's grasp to lap up some of the precious white stuff when a glass got a bit too close to his lips.

Now, we're not sure that dogs can benefit as much as people from the nine essential nutrients in every glass of milk, but Moose seemed to have a pretty big smile on his face.

The general populace isn't merely lacking culture, it's lacking calcium. In fact, 70% of men and 90% of women don't get enough. The enlightened among us, however, drink 3 glasses of milk a day. A practice that can prevent a Freudian condition known as "calcium envy."

got milk?

Curly **Howard**

When the Three Stooges arrived on the set, the typical knuckleheaded mayhem ensued. Moe sat down on a hacksaw, Larry got a couple of well-deserved finger pokes in the eye (he was the one who left the hacksaw on the chair), and Curly accidentally got his head caught in a vise.

Wouldn't it have been great if that's what actually happened? It would certainly have gone down in the annals of milk mustache lore as the absolute wackiest milk photo shoot of all time. We can dream, can't we?

What actually happened is that we were asked to come up with an ad that told people that the calcium in milk helped build strong bones.

After thinking about it a bit, we tried to come up with a list of celebrities who may have had the strongest bones of all time . . . and one name catapulted to the top of that list: Curly Howard.

He'd been hit, whacked, clobbered, and pulverized with every tool, building material, and medical instrument known to man . . . yet nothing could stop him. Did Curly have strong bones? Why, soitenly!

Nyuk, nyuk, nyuk!

Want strong bones?

Drinking enough milk helps keep bones strong
and may help prevent osteoporosis later.

got milk?

Jennifer Love **Hewitt**

When we photographed Jennifer Love Hewitt for this ad she was still starring in *Party of Five*. This was before *I Still Know What You Did Last Summer* and just after *I Know What You Did Last Summer*.

That, in a nutshell, is a brief list of Love's career highlights. ("Love" — that's what she asked us to call her at the photo shoot.)

Previous milk mustache celebrities included her *Party of Five* co-stars, Matthew Fox and Neve Campbell, which made Love feel real comfortable when she donned her white above-lip gloss.

We didn't actually shoot this photograph in Love's kitchen, although she said it really does look like that after she makes breakfast.

Love. We like that.

Who Wants To Be a Millionaire? Milk mustache questions have often been posed to contestants on game shows like *Jeopardy* and *Hollywood Squares* since the beginning of the campaign, but the first time we were mentioned on *Who Wants To Be a Millionaire*, even we were taken by surprise. Not by the question, as posed by host Regis Philbin, but by the answer from hot seat occupant, Jason Block.

Q: *"Which of the following have Joan Rivers, Spike Lee, and Dennis Rodman all worn for an ad campaign?*

A: Milk mustache; **B:** Wedding dress;
C: Hat topped with fruit; **D:** SCUBA gear."

A: "Regis, I know this one. It's actually one of the greatest advertising campaigns in history. I've got two words for you . . . 'got milk?' It's milk mustache . . . final answer."

That's advertising money can't buy.

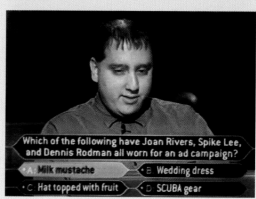

What does
Jennifer Love hate?

Osteoporosis.
So I drink fat free milk
with every meal. Each
glass has calcium to help
prevent it. Which makes
me feel good enough to
tackle something else
I hate: cleaning up.

got milk?

Everybody Loves Raymond
Cast

It was Ray Romano's idea.

On his hit television show, *Everybody Loves Raymond* he plays a character cleverly named Ray (good choice), a married father of three who lives across the street from his parents. His older brother Robert (played by Brad Garrett) is jealous of Ray's happy married life and charmed upbringing. Mom always did like Raymond best, and in most episodes of the show she continues to prove it.

We had planned to photograph the entire cast smiling happily in the camera with their milk mustaches until Ray said, "Wait a second. Everyone should have a milk mustache except for Robert. He shouldn't get any milk." We all laughed, and realized that was the way to go.

Not only did it play right into the sibling rivalry subplot of the show, but it gave us an opportunity to get a photograph of Brad doing what he does best . . . pouting.

TRACY ULLMAN
ALEX TREBEK

The many personalities of Tracy Ullman and Alex ("Can you put that in the form of a question?") Trebek from *Jeopardy*.

Share some calcium
with the ones you love.

Want strong bones?
Drinking enough lowfat milk now can help prevent osteoporosis later.
Assuming, of course, there's enough to go around.

got milk?

David **Boreanaz**

David Boreanaz rocketed to stardom playing Angel on *Buffy the Vampire Slayer*. His character was so popular with fans that he now has his own spinoff show titled (appropriately enough) *Angel*.

Since Angel is a "good vampire" (who even knew they existed?), we first tried photographing David hanging upside down by his feet on the ceiling like a bat.

In case you never tried it (and we certainly don't recommend that you do), hanging upside down from the ceiling by your feet like a bat is very, very uncomfortable. All the blood rushes to your head and, needless to say, we quickly abandoned this approach and decided to photograph David levitating in midair.

We suspended him in a dark, musty basement using a wired harness. The wires were removed by computer retouching later.

Just the right amount of smoke along with a narrow shaft of light entering from a small window created the perfect spooky environment for our hero.

And don't forget . . . milk is packed with nutrients and is certainly tastier than that other liquid vampires like to drink.

Watch your back.

Want strong bones?
Drinking enough lowfat
milk now can help prevent
osteoporosis later.
Now there's something to
sink your teeth into.

got milk?®

Erik Per **Sullivan**

"What are you guys making?"

"Chocolate milk for the photo shoot."

"Can I help?"

With those words, Erik Per Sullivan, Dewie of television's *Malcolm in the Middle*, became the first milk mustache celebrity to help make his own mustache.

Like any other eight-year-old would, Erik came running when he saw the chocolate syrup, mixing bowl, and kitchen utensils. With a big wooden spoon in one hand and a mixing bowl in the other, he slowly stirred the tasty mixture until it was ready for its closeup.

Most people don't realize that the milk mustaches we create for our ads (both white and chocolate) are not painted on or added after the photo session by computer trickery. Just about every celebrity since Naomi Campbell (our first) has gotten their milk mustache the same way you do: by drinking milk from a glass.

Sometimes the glass is small and sometimes it's big. Sometimes the milk is right out of the carton and sometimes it's thickened (with other dairy products) to be seen over, say, a man's mustache. Each milk mustache is applied by the celebrity from a glass in his or her own hand.

Now that you know, you can practice at home in front of the mirror.

Pages 22 and 23: Flexing their milk mustache muscles are **Frankie Muniz**, Malcolm himself, and WWF superstar **"Stone Cold" Steve Austin**.

They'll drink it if they know what's good for them. Chocolate milk has the same 9 essential nutrients as regular milk and is a more nutritious treat than soft drinks. Tell your kids. They're all ears.

got milk?®

Want strong kids?

Milk has nine essential
nutrients your kids'
active bodies need.
Which means you'd better
remember to save
some for yourself.

got milk?®

It better be ICE COLD
for STONE COLD.

Milk has nutrients active bodies need, and protein for butt-whoopin'
muscles. So make sure it's icy. 'Cause Stone Cold said so.

got milk?

Survivor **1**

When CBS first started airing *Survivor* in the summer of 2000, we saw an opportunity to associate milk with the hottest show on television. It was the show that everyone was watching and all of the media was talking about. Sensing that the finale was going to be a ratings bonanza, we designed "before and after" ads to run on the day of and the day after the last episode. In the "before" ad we showed the finalists; in the "after" ad we showed only the winner. The result: Not only was everyone talking about the *Survivor* finale, they were also talking about our ad. The press coverage of the Survivor milk ads was enormous. Every national morning show and many local news programs across the country were showing our ads.

In an unprecedented bit of coverage, our milk-mustache *Survivor* finalist photo was used as the front page of the New York *Daily News*. This was the first time an advertisement had ever appeared on the front page of that newspaper in its hundred-plus-year history.

As *Survivor* rapidly built to its fingernail-biting conclusion, everyone was asking the same question: "Would it be river guide Kelly Wiglesworth, ex-Navy SEAL Rudy Boesch, motivational speaker Richard Hatch, or truck driver Susan Hawk?" Everyone — including us . . .

What the last remaining survivor dreams of wearing tomorrow.

Want to win? Milk has nine essential nutrients active bodies need.

KELLY, RUDY, RICH & SUSAN ©2000 AMERICA'S DAIRY FARMERS AND MILK PROCESSORS

Rich **Hatch**

We had to photograph each of the four finalists in a celebratory pose and then watch the last episode of the show (along with all of the rest of America) to find out who won so that we could run our ad featuring the sole survivor the next day.

Even though the final show had yet to be aired, the filming had long been completed when we met Rudy, Kelly, Susan, and Rich on a deserted beach in Malibu to recreate their tropical island hut on the Malaysian island of Pulau Tiga.

We all wondered who had won. Surely one of them would give away the secret. Every few minutes we were sure we had it figured out.

"It's Kelly. She's so happy, and she exudes confidence. She must be the winner."

"Look over there. Rich is eating alone. Are the others jealous because he won the million dollars? It must be him."

"Did you overhear Rudy talking about getting signed with an agent? He's the obvious winner."

"Somebody said that Susan was in California all week. How can she afford to do that if she is still driving her truck? Maybe she's the one!"

But they were good. Real good. Truth be told, we had absolutely no idea who won. We were sitting on pins and needles like the other twenty-nine million viewers of the *Survivor* finale as Richard Hatch picked up his prize.

Kind of funny that the winner of the million dollars was named Rich, eh?

The strong survive.

got milk?®

Want to win? Milk has nine essential nutrients active bodies need.
And that makes everyone a winner. No matter how the tribal council votes.

Survivor 2

When CBS repeated its success with *Survivor II* in 2001, the decision to create a *Survivor II* milk mustache ad was a no brainer. This time it was set in the Australian outback, and rather than simply recreate the players' campsite again as we did in the previous *Survivor* ad, we chose to take a more creative path.

We came up with the idea of burying each of the three *Survivor* finalists up to their necks in sand as a make-believe last test of their stamina on the way to the million dollar prize.

We photographed professional chef Keith Famie, Tennessee mom Tina Wesson, and auto-detailer Colby Donaldson in New York City. We didn't actually bury the contestants in the sand (the scenery was added later), but we did shoot each of them in a real victory bubble bath for the winner ad.

The last survivor standing (or in this case, bathing) was Tina Wesson, who triumphed over Colby in the final round of the game.

Once again, we had no idea who the actual winner would be when we photographed the bubble bath ads, but we were pretty confident that Colby would win . . . so go figure.

Tina Wesson

got milk?

Athletes are perfect for the milk campaign. Because of milk's nine essential nutrients, it is something that every athlete needs in his or her diet. Since milk is on the training table of most sports trainers and athletes, it's very easy to get athletes to be in the milk campaign. If these healthy, strong, active people, who depend on the performance of their bodies drink milk, imagine what it can do for you. Here are the latest athletes, who join previous milk mustache sports personalities like Pete Sampras, Patrick Ewing, and Oscar De La Hoya in the campaign.

Mark McGwire

We contacted Mark McGwire in the summer of '98 when all of the world was focused on just one thing: Roger Maris' all-time record of 61 home runs in one season. Mark's agent said that Mark wasn't talking to anyone until after the season was over. We were told to check back with him then.

So we waited and we watched as he tied Maris' record of 61 home runs on Labor Day and when he broke it seven days later with number 62.

But he didn't stop there.

Home runs number 63, 64, 65, 66, 67, and 68 followed. Then, on Mark's last day at bat, on September 27, 1998, he rocked the world by hitting two more . . . numbers 69 and 70.

That's when we made our second call, and Mark McGwire said, "Yes."

It should be noted that around this time Mark McGwire was quite possibly the most celebrated man in America. Offers for advertisers and endorsers poured in from coast to coast. Yet he was very selective, and chose to do just a few things that he deemed close to his heart. The Milk Mustache Campaign was one of them.

"I want to do it for the kids," he said.

It was Mark's idea not to be in uniform for his portrait. He didn't want his ad to be about Major League Baseball or the St. Louis Cardinals. He wanted it to be simple: a portrait of a man, a bat, and a dream.

A dream that most certainly came true.

Going, going, gone.

Time for more milk. It's got stuff leading sports drinks don't—
like protein, potassium and calcium. That's why I always have
an ice-cold glass...as soon as I get home.

got milk?

Kevin **Garnett**

If you're a fan of Minnesota Timberwolves superstar Kevin Garnett, you should recognize that face.

You know, the face with the mouth in mid-roar that you see on television and in the sports magazines when Kevin is barreling past a couple of defenders or hanging from the basket by both hands just after he slam dunks a winning basket.

Yes . . . that face.

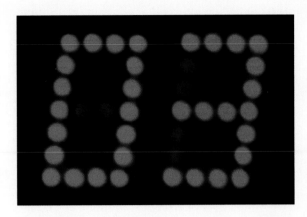

glasses a day

got milk?®

We did a regular magazine print ad with Kevin as well as the outdoor billboard advertisement pictured here.

His intensity on the court is legendary, and proved to be the perfect complement to his milk mustache as he ferociously posed for our camera.

"I drink milk every day because it helps make my bones strong," Kevin explained. "I definitely stress nutrition. As a pro athlete you have to take care of your body."

So, does Kevin "got milk?" Read his lips.

Coaches

Joe Torre has led the New York Yankees to an impressive number of American League and World Series championships.

In 1999, Jeff Fisher led the Tennessee Titans to within a yard of a possible Super Bowl victory and became only the fifth coach in NFL history to lead his team to consecutive thirteen-win seasons.

Pat Riley, the current head coach of the Miami Heat, led the L.A. Lakers to four World Championships and in the process became the all-time winningest percentage head coach in NBA history.

Each coach is unquestionably among the best in his respective game. So how did we manage to get the top three coaches of the top three sports in America in one locker room at the same time? The answer is . . . we didn't.

We built a mobile locker room set and photographed Jeff Fisher and Joe Torre together one afternoon in Ft. Lauderdale, FL. Then we loaded the set onto a truck and drove it to Miami where Pat Riley was photographed alone, leaving room for where Joe and Jeff would be positioned.

With Joe, Jeff, and Pat's combined records we knew that this milk mustache ad would be a winner.

TERRELL DAVIS
Denver Broncos Running Back Terrell Davis with his uniform painted onto his muscular frame

Want muscle?

Milk has protein to help build muscle.

got milk?

Want to play?

Milk has 9 essential nutrients that active bodies need.
Which makes milk, as we say in the business, a "good call."

got milk?

WN**BA**

The WNBA was only two years old in 1999, but some of it's superstar players were already household names.

Nikki McCray of the Washington Mystics, Lisa Leslie of the Los Angeles Sparks, and Sheryl Swoopes of the Houston Comets had already made names for themselves at the 1996 Olympic Games where they helped the U.S. women's basketball team beat Brazil 111–87.

The Gold Medal-Winning trio was reunited for our milk mustache photo.

So how did we decide which of the top players would get the honor of spinning the milk glass on her finger like a basketball? Simple. We gave it to the one standing in the middle.

It was amazing to see how easily Lisa balanced the milk-filled glass on her fingertip, even after posing for at least a hundred photos.

She never spilled a drop.

Pages 38 and 39: Soccer superstar **Mia Hamm** (showing how she can handle a glass of milk) and one of the fastest women alive, **Marion Jones**. Wanna take her on?

9 essential nutrients.

Want game?
Milk is packed with vitamins
and minerals that active
bodies need.

got milk?

MIA HAMM ©1999 AMERICA'S DAIRY FARMERS AND MILK PROCESSORS

Wanna race?
Milk has nine
essential nutrients
active bodies need.
It can't be beat.
And neither can I.

got milk?®

Rulon **Gardner**

One athlete who knows the value of milk is Olympic champion Rulon Gardner. Turns out the Greco-Roman wrestler who captured the gold medal and hearts of millions at the Summer Olympics in Sydney is a Wyoming dairy farmer.

The youngest of nine children, Rulon grew up hauling five-gallon buckets of milk at the family farm.

"Long hours of training helped me win an Olympic gold medal, but endurance was critical," said Gardner. "I wouldn't have made it through training and the match without the right fuel in my tank. Milk was a key part of my training diet."

Rulon, one of the sweetest guys you'll ever meet, entertained everyone at the photo shoot with stories of his Wyoming farm life. He even entertained the cow.

Seems growing up on a farm means you spend so much time listening to cows that you start believing you can speak their language. Rulon does. By cupping his hands over his mouth and mooing, he can actually speak "cow."

At least that's what he claimed.

To us it sounded something like, "Mooo. Mooooooooooo. Mooooo." What the cow heard, well, that's anyone's guess.

Gardner's milk mustache ad made its debut in *Sports Illustrated*'s year-end "Sportsman of the Year" issue a few months after his triumph at the Olympics.

Mooo, indeed.

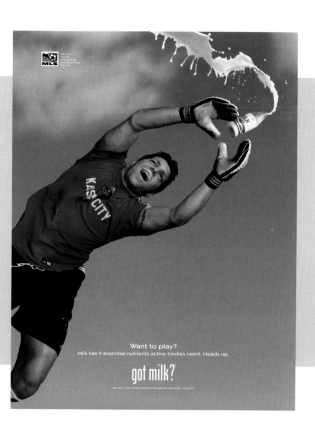

TONY MEOLA
Kansas City Wizards goalkeeper Tony Meola making an impressive midair save.

Dairy King.
Want to win? Milk has 9 essential nutrients active bodies need.
Growing up on a dairy farm didn't hurt either.

got milk?

Mat **Hoffman**

When we found out that ten-time World Vertical BMX Bike Champion Mat Hoffman wanted to do a chocolate milk mustache ad we knew exactly what we wanted to do: Photograph him relaxing on his living room sofa holding a big glass of chocolate milk.

Yeah . . . right!

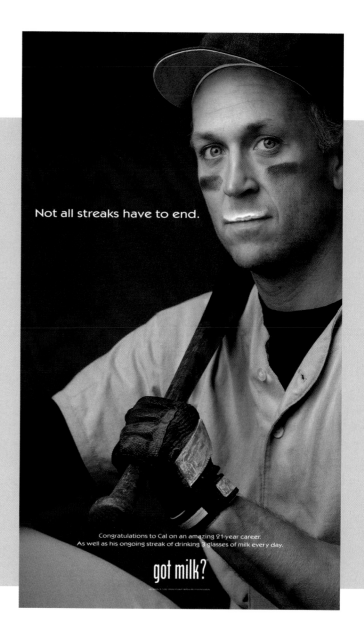

CAL RIPKEN This ad was created in honor of the retirement of Baltimore Orioles legend Cal Ripken.

Great taste. Strong bones.
Why wouldn't you risk your neck for it?

got chocolate milk?

SUPERBOWL XXXIII

Continuing a tradition that began in 1997, we create a milk mustache ad to commemorate each Super Bowl. While many advertisers run ads on the Super Bowl telecast, we are the only advertiser that actually features opposing team members in an ad prior to the game. Then on the Monday morning after the big game, the winning quarterback is already in his own milk mustache ad.

Atlanta Falcons quarterback Chris Chandler was prepared to take the crown away from returning Super Bowl champion and MVP John Elway . . . but the Denver Bronco superstar wasn't ready to give up the spotlight.

Playing in the final game of his long NFL career, Elway crushed the Falcons 34–19 and was named Super Bowl MVP for the second time in a row, assuring him of a spot in the football Hall of Fame.

But for Elway, a spot on his daughter's "Wall of Fame" was made possible by milk: "My daughter collects the milk campaign advertising . . . and she hangs them on her wall. When I told her I was going to be involved in the milk campaign, she was all excited and I was glad to make her wall."

So were we.

44

It's not just a milk mustache. It's also a winning streak.

got milk?

SUPERBOWL **XXXIV**

Before the big game, St. Louis Rams quarterback Kurt Warner fought Tennessee Titans quarterback Steve McNair for a prized quart of the white stuff. In a photo finish (one yard shy of a Super Bowl winning touchdown) McNair was sent to the locker room to sulk while Warner smiled all the way to the dairy aisle.

We're usually forced by schedules and limited time to shoot each quarterback for our Super Bowl milk mustache ads separately in their hometown. The two photos are then combined digitally into one for the final ad. This was the first time both quarterbacks were photographed together at the exact same time. We were told it might have been the first time that two Super Bowl quarterbacks were photographed together before the big game . . . ever!

Now isn't that something.

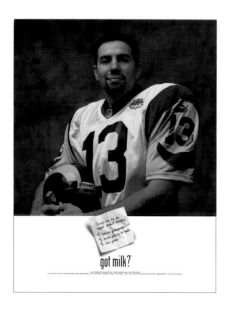

KURT WARNER

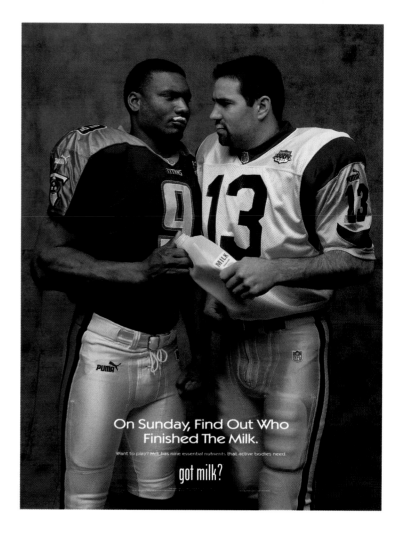

On Sunday, Find Out Who Finished The Milk.

got milk?

SUPERBOWL **XXXV**

We were once again back to shooting both players separately for this milk mustache portrait.

New York Giants quarterback Kerry Collins and Baltimore Ravens quarterback Trent Dilfer were pictured squaring off before the big game in Tampa, Florida. Both players were confident, secure, and truly believed they had what it would take to win the biggest game of their lives.

But it's the final score that does the talking. And in the end Dilfer wiped the milk mustache off Collins' face in a 34–7 rout.

TRENT DILFER

ANIMATED CHARACTERS

Once we started to gear our ads more toward young people, using animated and cartoon characters was a natural. The first animated characters to ever wear milk mustaches were Bart and Lisa Simpson. Since then, some of the greatest superheroes and television characters have joined them.

Super**man**

Look! Up in the sky! It's a bird! It's a plane! It's . . . Milkman?

Everyone knows that the first and possibly most popular superhero of all time can be hurt by kryptonite. But what is the source of his power?

If only we knew . . .

Pages 50 and 51: Two Marvel Comics superheroes, the Incredible Hulk and the Amazing Spider-Man.

The calcium in milk
helps make bones strong.

got milk?

Kermit the **Frog**

Our first meeting with Kermit the Frog was at Muppet Headquarters in the heart of Manhattan.

We entered a spacious, mahogany-paneled boardroom and took our seats around an equally impressive conference room table. Over a seat at the head of the table was a fine, ornately framed painting of Kermit, looking down with authority from the hallowed walls of these very prestigious trappings.

After a few awkward minutes of silence, the door opened. And in came a man carrying a cardboard box. Inside the box was Kermit himself.

A rather unimpressive entrance from such an impressive character, we thought.

But Kermit would eventually win the day. By donning his favorite designer suit and enchanting us all with his lily pad wit, he proved that he was indeed a frog with style.

Milk isn't just for tadpoles.

Did you know 3 out of 4 adults don't get enough calcium?
It takes at least 3 glasses of milk a day. I always keep some at my pad.

got milk?

The **Rugrats**

Kids like Rugrats. Rugrats like milk. Kids see Rugrats liking milk. Kids like milk. Seems like that would work. Actually, it worked so well that we did it twice.

Our initial ad was based on the Rugrats' first feature-length movie, titled appropriately enough, *The Rugrats Movie*. The babies' first feature film was number one at the box office its first week out. Their follow-up film, *The Rugrats in Paris*, was a hit, too . . . and so was our second milk mustache ad. This one featured Tommy, Chuckie, and their dads.

Did it work the second time around? Oui, oui.

RUGRATS IN PARIS

"Chuckie, why do you think they call 'em growed-ups?"

Want your kids to grow? The calcium in milk helps your bones grow strong.
So give them a tall glass. Then move the cookie jar to the next shelf.

got milk?®

Bat**man**

As everyone who reads comic books knows, Batman, Gotham City's caped crusader is also known as the Dark Knight.

So, what better to fill the fridge at stately Wayne Manor or the Batcave than with chilled bottles of delicious chocolate milk?

After all, chocolate milk has all the same nutrients as regular milk, plus the added advantage of giving the drinker a dark brown milk mustache.

Plus, milk's calcium for strong bones comes in handy for superheroes wherever and whenever duty calls. It's also pretty good for us regular folks, too.

As his faithful ward and canary-yellow-tights-wearing sidekick Robin might say, "Holy best source of calcium, Batman!"

BLUE'S CLUES
This ad features Steve from *Blue's Clues* (having a hard time deciding between chocolate and regular milk) and his puppy, Blue (who has already decided.)

Be a Dark Knight.

Want to grow?
Chocolate milk has all the nutrients
of regular milk, so drink up.

got milk?

Garfield the **Cat**

Halfway through our meeting with the creators of Garfield the Cat, we had reached an impasse. Our copy was being scrutinized by the Garfield powers-that-be.

"Garfield the Cat wouldn't say that," they said.

"But Garfield the Cat isn't real," we said. Which was met by stunned silence on the other end of the phone.

What were we thinking? Of course Garfield is real. As real as anything in this world that could employ a whole building full of people trying to figure out what a drawing of a cat with a milk mustache would say.

And who are we to quibble anyway? We've got a whole building of people trying to write the words that a drawing of a cat with a milk mustache would say.

**HI AND LOIS
THE FAMILY CIRCUS**

From *Saturday Night Live* to *Mad* magazine . . . over the years, we've had many television shows, magazines, newspapers, and movies get smiles from their audiences using our Milk Mustache Campaign.

Here are two comic strips with a similar theme. Read these strips, then read their lips.

Lazy bones? Ha! My bones are growing. 'Cause I lap up fat free milk. You should, too. Calcium helps your bones grow until about age 35. After that, it helps keep them strong. Plus, nothing goes better with lasagna. Would you mind spoon-feeding me?

got milk?®

The Powerpuff **Girls**

Created by Professor Utonium by combining sugar, spice, and everything nice along with the mysterious "Chemical X," the Powerpuff Girls are superheroes unlike any other. They fly into action whenever the city of Townsville is in trouble, fighting crime, punishing nefarious villains, and saving the day . . . all before bedtime.

Each member of the heroic trio has her own super powers and favorite flavor of milk.

Bubbles likes banana-flavored milk. It's yummy and is the same color as her hair.

Blossom, the leader of the group, wouldn't think of drinking anything but strawberry milk. It really packs a punch.

And as for Buttercup, well . . . we think her comments speak for themselves: "Chocolate milk kicks butt!"

Well said, Buttercup, well said.

PIKACHU
Pikachu has milk power
— do you?

Milk Power.

got milk?

Want to grow? Drinking milk helps your bones grow
so you can evolve to the next level.

©2000 AMERICA'S DAIRY FARMERS AND MILK PROCESSORS. PIKACHU ©2000 Nintendo/ Creatures inc./GAME FREAK inc.

Powerpuff power.

Banana, chocolate and strawberry
milks are tasty and yummy with vitamins
and minerals to help you play hard.
Once again, the day is saved.

got milk?®

Super Mario

This milk mustache ad started out as a television commercial.

Two kids are sitting on their living room floor playing Super Mario. They are having a hard time getting him over an obstacle when Mom calls them for dinner.

Once the kids have left the room, Mario pops out of the TV set. He hops on a skateboard, bounces over a sofa, and avoids the claws of the pet cat to reach his goal: an ice cold gulp of milk from a gallon jug. He grows instantly, which allows him to jump back into the game and climb over the obstacle in his path.

After we saw how great the TV commercial came out, we quickly signed Mario up for his own milk mustache print ad.

"Mama mia!"

SPONGEBOB SQUAREPANTS

Nickelodeon's popular cartoon character SpongeBob SquarePants learns the hard way that a sponge can't enjoy the simple pleasure of a chocolate milk mustache.

Milk mustaches don't last long when you're a sponge.

Which means I may have to drink another glass of yummy chocolate milk.

Or two.

Or three.

Or four.

Power Up!

Want to grow?
The calcium in milk
helps your bones grow.
Momma Mia!

got milk?®

MUSIC

If you are going to have a celebrity campaign that tries to reach teenagers, the music business is hard to ignore. But picking the music stars that are going to be around for a while versus the "one-hit wonders" is tricky. Take a look at how we did.

The Backstreet Boys

They were the biggest recording group in the world when we assembled Nick, Kevin, A.J., Brian, and Howie D. on the backstreets of lower Manhattan that day.

Security was super tight. But it's hard to keep a secret in New York City, and before long a couple dozen onlookers had gathered to watch. A number of them, clutching copies of the Backstreet Boys first multiplatinum CD, were obviously hoping for autographs from the boys in the band.

Brian brought along his pet chihuahua, Lil' Tyke, who was curiously checking out all of the makeup stylists, photo assistants, and public relations people who attended the photo shoot. It takes a lot of support people to shoot one milk mustache photo, especially when you're photographing some of the most popular singers on the planet.

Each member of the band had their own hair and makeup person, and it shows.

Come to think of it, did a milk mustache ever look that cute when it was on your brother's lip as you laughed at him across the kitchen table at breakfast?

We didn't think so.

It takes more
than a hit single to
reach the top.

15% of adult height is added during teen years. So we
give our growing bones lots of calcium by drinking milk. How do
you suppose we reach all those high notes, anyway?

got milk?®

The Dixie **Chicks**

For their milk mustache portrait, the Dixie Chicks wanted to be photographed milking a cow. So we got a cow. What we didn't know was that the cow had just given birth to a cute little calf.

One look at her sweet face, and it was love at first sight for Emily Robison, Natalie Maines, and Martie Seidel.

The calf was so new to the world that she didn't even have a name . . . so Natalie christened her "Loretta."

Emily, Natalie, and Martie posed for a number of photographs with the calf's mom, but their attention kept being drawn to Loretta, who was never too far away.

We asked the country superstar trio if they wanted to take a few photos with Loretta, and after changing into a matching set of hip-hugger boots, they were ready.

Now, a baby calf may look pretty small in comparison to her farm-sized mom, but take it from us — she was quite a handful . . . especially for Natalie.

"I've never been the typical farm girl," Natalie said. "That cow was really heavy, though."

The Dixie Chicks (and Loretta) were nominated for a 2001 Country Weekly Music Award in honor of their milk mustache debut.

Great for growing chicks.

Want strong bones?
Your bones grow until about
age 35 and the calcium in
milk helps. After that,
it helps keep them strong.
Chicks rule.

got milk?

Carson Daly

We photographed Carson Daly at MTV studios in New York City right in front of the big-screen television monitor used to show each of the weekly *Total Request Live* countdown videos.

One of the things you may not know about photographing celebrities for ads like the milk mustache campaign is that every single detail of a photograph has to be discussed and approved by a number of talented people before it ever reaches a magazine. Location, lighting, background, pose, props, hairstyle, makeup, wardrobe . . . the list goes on and on.

We even have meetings where we discuss the size of the glass in the celebrity's hand.

When we shot Carson on the set of *TRL*, we had him change into three or four outfits before choosing the clothing we ultimately used. Highly skilled stylists (with a flair for fashion) help us decide what's best for each performer and situation. If you look at our photo and think, "This just looks like something I'd see on MTV," it means we did a good job.

Don't you wish you had a stylist to help pick out your clothes?

Check out Latin heartthrob **Marc Anthony.**

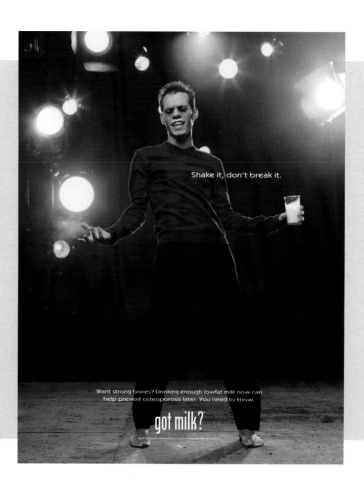

got milk?®

PHILIPS

01 Hey everybody! Want to grow? About 15% of your height is added during your teen years and milk can help make the most of it. That's why it's #1. Milk rocks!   > Carson

Kiss

Kiss first burst onto the music scene in 1974. With their painted faces and eccentric stage theatrics, they were a smash sensation. Almost thirty years later, Kiss continues to sell out arena-sized stadiums worldwide.

Gene Simmons was the first to arrive on set for our photo shoot. He wanted to experiment with the chocolate milk mixture. We hoped to have him showcase his world-famous tongue in action in our photo and he didn't disappoint us.

The other members of the band, Peter Criss, Paul Stanley, and Ace Frehley soon joined their bandmate in full Kiss regalia.

Gene asked us where the ad was scheduled to run. We told him, "the big music magazines, *Rolling Stone, Spin* . . ." We laughed as we added, "We're not going to run the ad in *Better Homes and Gardens* or *Woman's Day*."

Gene didn't laugh.

Instead he said with a straight face, "Let me tell you why you should run our ad in *Better Homes and Gardens* and *Woman's Day*. Daddy is a fan of Kiss. Mommy is a fan of Kiss. Little Johnny is a fan of Kiss. We have more generations of fans that love Kiss than you can imagine."

It's no wonder that they're still one of the hottest bands in the world thirty years after they started.

Note: The ad still hasn't run in *Better Homes and Gardens* or *Woman's Day,* but we hear there may be another Kiss album coming out, so you never know.

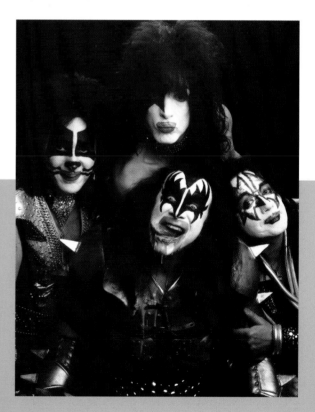

Lick it up.

After rock and rolling all night, we need nourishment. And every
drop of chocolate milk has the same vitamins and minerals regular milk has.
All the more reason to have a really, really long tongue.

got milk?®

Elton **John**

"Elton John is in his limousine."
"Elton John is two blocks away from the studio."
"Elton John is in the parking lot."
"Elton John has arrived."

With a flurry of cell phone calls, David LaChapelle was less than an hour away from photographing Elton John for his milk mustache premiere.

Elton was in the building.

We wanted to photograph him wearing one of the flamboyantly colorful outfits he's known for in a completely white set. White room, white piano, white candelabra, white sculptures adorning the wall, and you guessed it . . . white milk.

Elton didn't just bring one multicolored suit to the set. He brought a rack of them. All Versace originals . . . all exactly the same pattern of big polka dots of varying colors. We chose the pink polka dots on tangerine ("Excellent choice," he said).

We decided in the interest of time to forgo applying a milk mustache to Elton on the set, thinking we could easily add it later by retouching. But as we escorted Elton to his piano, he turned and said, "Wait a minute. Where's my milk mustache?" We explained to him that we didn't think he wanted to be bothered with it, but he insisted.

"I want a milk mustache," he exclaimed.

And so, with glass in hand, Sir Elton got his milk mustache. And we got our photo.

A few days later, Elton made a well-publicized appearance on the Grammy Awards. As he crossed the stage and sat down at his piano to the roaring applause of the crowd, one thing jumped out at us: a familiar tangerine suit with pink polka dots.

Excellent choice.

Note: Sir Elton John is not only the first milk mustache celebrity to have been knighted, he's also the first milk mustache celebrity to have won an Oscar, Grammy, and Tony award.

I'm still standing.

Want strong bones?
Drinking enough
lowfat milk
now can help prevent
osteoporosis later.

got milk?®

Britney Spears

We are constantly watching celebrities and trying to predict who is going to be hot, so we pride ourselves in catching celebrities whose stars are on the rise. When Britney Spears had just arrived on the scene with her first hit single, we identified her as the girl singer who was going to have the most staying power.

She also loved to drink milk.

"On the airplane and in the morning," Britney told us. "I'm a really big milk drinker. I'm always drinking milk, I really am. It's really important being on the road and everything that you have the right vitamins and minerals in your body...to have energy and everything. I think it's really important."

We did our first ad with her in 1999. "Baby One More Time" had just skyrocketed to the top of the charts. We photographed Britney in a stylized purple bedroom talking on the phone with a plate of milk and cookies by her side. She had just injured her leg while filming a music video and arrived on the set on crutches.

We were a little nervous about how easily she'd be able to handle posing on the retro-style chair chosen for the photo shoot, but she handled it like a real pro.

We knew there were big things in store for Britney. We just couldn't have imagined how big.

When we asked Britney which milk ad was her favorite she said, "I really like Jennifer Love Hewitt's. Hers was really cool with the pancakes and everything. It was really natural. I thought it was hot. [And] the Backstreet Boys, theirs was really cool. Hopefully they will dig mine as much as I dig theirs."

After her first album hit the top of the charts, Britney had a makeover. Just about everything changed, except for her love of milk.

**Baby,
one more time
isn't enough.**

9 out of 10 girls don't
get enough calcium. It takes
about 4 glasses of milk
every day. So when I finish
this glass, fill it up, baby.
Three more times.

got milk?

BRITNEY SPEARS ©1999 NATIONAL FLUID MILK PROCESSOR PROMOTION BOARD

Britney **Spears**

Britney became so popular that we shot a second ad in 2000 to celebrate the fact that Milk was the title sponsor of her summer tour. The tour was called, "Got Milk presents Britney Spears."

According to Britney, "My manager called and said, 'Milk is sponsoring your tour!' I was like, 'How cool is that?' I was really happy when he told me."

Britney was only the second celebrity to appear in more than one regular milk mustache ad. The first was supermodel Christie Brinkley, who made her first appearance as one of the original five ads that launched the campaign. Christie appeared again, the next year with her children Alexa Ray and Jack Paris.

For Britney's second milk mustache ad we wanted to capture a hipper, cooler Britney whose image had changed dramatically from the sweet innocence of her earlier days.

We did two ads. One featured Britney as a teenager standing next to herself as a child. Britney's mom supplied the photo of Britney in her tutu (age 5) and we supplied the milk.

The second ad showcased Britney and a spilled stream of milk caught in midair by the photographer's flash as it danced across the page.

The set (and Britney) was completely soaked with milk by the time we were done with the photo session. Don't worry, though. We made sure we got enough dry shots of her for the summer tour promotion before the milk started flying.

Grow up.

Want to grow?
15% of your height is
added during your teen
years and milk can help
make the most of it.

got milk?

MORE STARS

Some stars aren't easily categorized. They do it all. Here are a few more celebrities that have joined the ranks of past stars like Spike Lee, Danny DeVito, and Martha Stewart.

Jackie Chan

Everyone knows that Jackie Chan does his own stunts…so did photographer David LaChapelle just happen to be walking down a street in downtown Los Angeles with his camera at the exact moment that Jackie was making a daring escape on a rope ladder attached to the bottom of a rescue helicopter after downing a quart of milk?

You won't get it out of us. But we should mention that Jackie could never have survived if it weren't for his very, very, very strong bones.

Real Name:
Chan Kwong Sang
Date of Birth:
April 7, 1954
Place of Birth:
Hong Kong
Favorite Beverage:
Milk

Mike **Myers**

We traveled to Hollywood for our photo shoot with Mike Myers on the set of *Austin Powers: The Spy Who Shagged Me*. The first movie had been such a huge success that when the studio called and asked if we wanted to do a milk mustache tie-in to the sequel, we thought it was shagadelic!

Our original idea was to photograph Mike Myers as both Austin Powers and Austin's arch-nemesis Dr. Evil. The two were to be pictured side by side in the ad.

But just before we arrived for the shoot, we were informed that the Dr. Evil makeup took so long to apply that Mike wouldn't be able to do both characters in one day. So we decided to just photograph Austin Powers.

The day we visited the set, Mike and Heather Graham were filming scenes in Austin's psychedelic bachelor pad. We arrived at around one P.M. and were told that we could take our photo as soon as they finished shooting for the day. Expecting a few hours delay, we waited. And waited. And waited.

They didn't actually finish shooting until a full twelve hours later! Half-expecting Mike Myers to be completely exhausted after so many hours of filming, we were startled by the fact that not only was he quite energized and enthusiastic, but that he remained in character for the entire photo shoot.

That's right. It was as if we were actually photographing Austin Powers for a milk mustache ad instead of Mike Myers.

"Can you turn a little bit to the left, Mike?"

"Ab-so-lute-ly, my darling. Are you getting my good side? Smashing! How's this? Yeah, baby. Yeah!"

At one point, Mike actually broke character to laugh at one of his own jokes. Along with all of us.

What's my bag?
It's milk, baby, yeah!
The calcium in lowfat or fat free milk helps to prevent osteoporosis and keep my bones strong. So I can keep my mojo working overtime. Oh, *behave*.
got milk?®
"AUSTIN POWERS™: THE SPY WHO SHAGGED ME." ©1999 NEW LINE PRODUCTIONS, INC. ALL RIGHTS RESERVED.
©1999 NATIONAL FLUID MILK PROCESSOR PROMOTION BOARD

Whoopi **Goldberg**

We asked Whoopi Goldberg to be one of our first milk mustache celebrities in the early days of the campaign but she had to turn us down. She told us that although she loved the ads, she couldn't drink milk because she was lactose intolerant.

Imagine her surprise when we called a couple of years later to ask if she would be interested in being in the campaign *because* she was lactose intolerant! We wanted to feature her in an ad for lactose-free milk.

This time she said, "Yes."

SARAH MICHELLE GELLAR
Sarah was one of the first television stars to wear a milk mustache when we photographed her as Buffy the Vampire Slayer. Check out this locker-poster that ran once in a special issue of *TV Guide*.

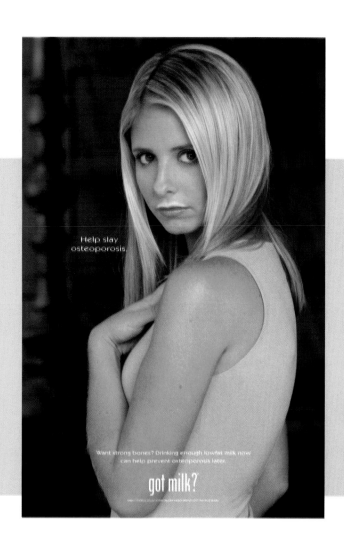

Help slay osteoporosis.

Want strong bones? Drinking enough lowfat milk now can help prevent osteoporosis later.

got milk?

Hear the
one about the
comedian who
never drank
milk?

She had a
weak funny bone.
Lucky for us
lactose-intolerant
folks, there's
lactose-free milk.
It's available
everywhere, and
it has all the calcium
of regular milk.
Good thing. I'm here
to crack you up —
not myself.

got milk?®

Melanie **Griffith**

Everybody knows Melanie Griffith is a great actress, but she's also a great mom.

We photographed Melanie Griffith along with her three children: Alexander, Dakota, and Stella lounging next to a large built-in swimming pool in Southern California. No, it's not her pool (although we're pretty sure that hers is just as nice).

All three children were really well behaved, including baby Dakota, who made it a habit of never traveling anywhere without her bottle . . . filled to the rim with milk, of course.

While we were photographing Melanie and her family a man who happened to be jogging by stopped to watch. Before long, all eyes were on him instead of Melanie. Why is that? Simple. The jogger was Mel Gibson.

The Mel Gibson!

After watching for a few minutes, he continued on his way.

At the end of the photo shoot, we were left with one unanswered question:

Can you get a milk mustache by drinking milk from a bottle? Since Dakota never took it out of her mouth for long, we'll never know.

Mom Melanie doesn't have to tell her kids to "drink your milk!" They already do.

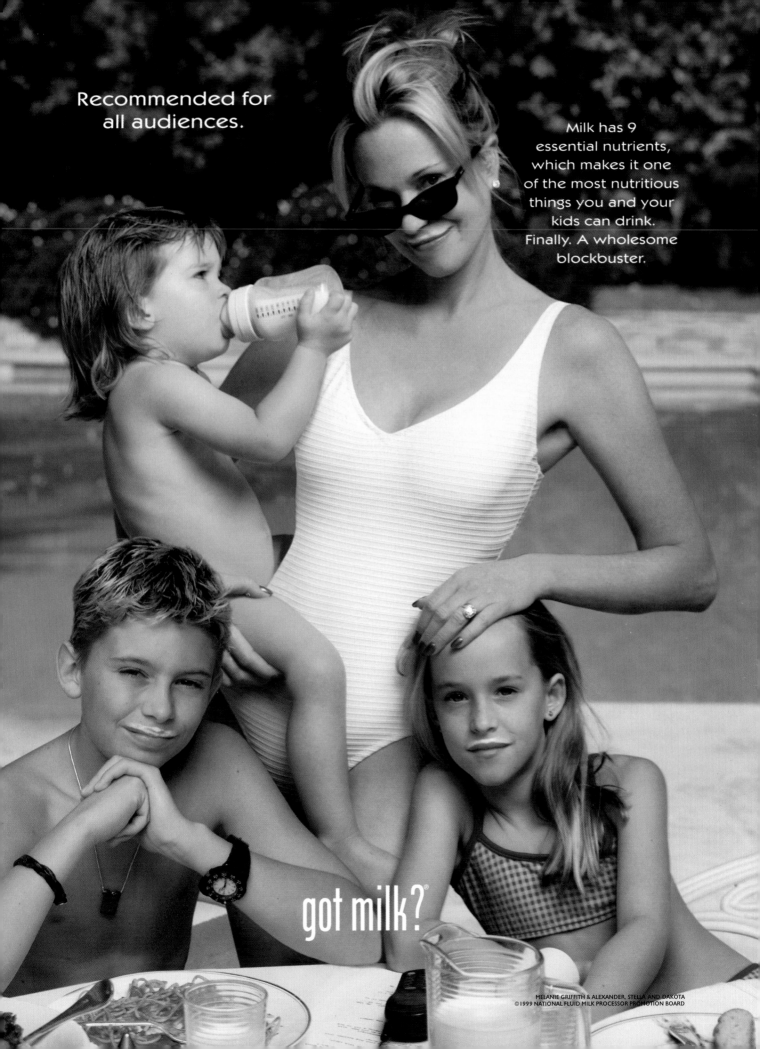

Recommended for all audiences.

Milk has 9 essential nutrients, which makes it one of the most nutritious things you and your kids can drink. Finally. A wholesome blockbuster.

got milk?

Ronald **McDonald**

Trying to figure out how he would look best with his milk mustache at the photo shoot, we asked Ronald if he liked to smile with his mouth open or closed? He responded, "I like to smile whatever way you want me to smile. That's what I like to do best."

That certainly made us smile. And made one thing abundantly clear . . . if everyone in the world was as happy and carefree as Ronald McDonald, the world would surely be a better place.

And we'd all be able to get fries on demand, twenty-four hours a day.

Ronald loves milk because it makes him grow from head to toe!

Want to grow?

got milk?®

Super Size

Medium

Small

Election **Ad**

The Florida recount headlines just about wrote this ad for us. Everyone in the country was talking about it…and, as they say, timing is everything.

With all eyes on the 2000 presidential election recount, we thought it would be fun to add our own bit of tongue-in-cheek humor.

So we created our election tribute ad to remind people about the importance of good nutrition, and in the process, hopefully put a milk mustache as well as a smile on everyone's lips.

THE MILK HOUSE

All around the country, kids are competing at the local level in a variety of sports with the hope of joining their teammates at Disney's Wide World of Sports™ Complex at the Walt Disney World® Resort in Lake Buena Vista, Florida.

When they get there, their first stop will be the Milk House, a 54,000-square-foot facility proudly sponsored by milk and decorated with milk mustache sports celebrity portraits. If your team is lucky enough to make it to the finals, maybe you'll pose for your very own milk mustache photo!

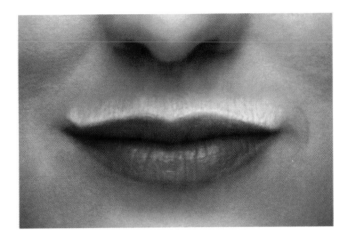

9 Essential Nutrients.
(We recounted them just to be sure.)

Want to win?
Milk has nine essential nutrients active bodies need.
Which means you'll come out ahead.
Every time.

Contest **Winner**

Since the Milk Mustache Campaign began, we've been deluged with photos, letters, and e-mails from people asking to be in an ad. While we've rarely featured non-celebrities, we have regularly run ads that feature contest winners, like Cherish Wise whose milk ad ran in *Seventeen* magazine in 2001.

MAKE-A-WISH

When the Make-A-Wish Foundation found out that Courtney (who was diagnosed with leukemia) wanted to be in a milk mustache ad, they called us…and we helped make her wish come true.

Index

Photo and Illustration Credits

Batman Ad

Batman, Dark Knight and all related characters, names and indicia are trademarks of DC Comics © 2000.

Superman Ad

Superman Man of Steel and all related characters, names and indicia are trademarks of DC Comics © 2000

Garfield Ad

PHOTOGRAPHY: COLIN COOKE
© Paws 1998

Frasier **Ad**

PHOTOGRAPHY: RICHARD CORMAN

Pikachu Ad

© 2000 Nintendo/Creatures Inc./GAME FREAK Inc.

Mario Ad

PHOTOGRAPHY: CRAIG CUTLER
Mario character © 2000 Nintendo of America Inc. All Rights Reserved.

Curly Howard Ad

PHOTOGRAPHY: STEVE HELLERSTEIN
™ & ©1999 C3 ENTERTAINMENT, INC.

Kermit Ad

KERMIT THE FROG™ & ©HENSON 1999

Blue's Clues **Ad**

2000 Viacom International, Inc. All Rights Reserved. Nickelodeon, Blue's Clues and all related titles, characters and logos are trademarks of Viacom International, Inc.

Superbowl Ads

PHOTOGRAPHY: WALTER IOOSS, JR.

The NFL and the NFL shield are registered trademarks of the National Football League. Team names, logos and uniform designs are registered trademarks of the teams indicated.

Elton John, Kevin Garnett, Jackie Chan and *Survivor I* **Ads**

PHOTOGRAPHY: DAVID LACHAPELLE

Hulk Ad

Hulk TM © 1999 Marvel Characters, Inc.

Spider-Man Ad

Spider-Man TM © 1999 Marvel Characters, Inc.

Mat Hoffman Ad

PHOTOGRAPHY: LUIS SANCHIS

Seventeen **Winner Ad**

PHOTOGRAPHY: Carlo Dalla Chiessa

Election Ad

PHOTOGRAPHY: ANDY SPREITZER

Survivor II **Ads**

PHOTOGRAPHY: SACHA WALDMAN

Rugrats **Ads**

Nickelodeon, RUGRATS and all related titles, logos and characters are trademarks of Viacom International Inc. RUGRATS created by ARLENE KLASKY, GABOR CSUPO and PAUL GERMAIN. Copyright © 1998 & 2000 by PARAMOUNT PICTURES and VIACOM INTERNATIONAL INC. All Rights Reserved.

Ronald McDonald Ad

© 2001 McDonald's Corporation. The golden arches logo, Ronald McDonald and super size are trademarks of McDonald's Corporation and its affiliates.

The Powerpuff Girls Ad

The Powerpuff Girls and all related characters and elements are trademarks of Cartoon Network © 2001

SpongeBob SquarePants Ad

© 2001 Viacom International Inc. All Rights Reserved. Nickelodeon, SpongeBob SquarePants and all related titles, logos and SpongeBob SquarePants created by Stephen Hillenburg.

All other ads photographed by

ANNIE LEIBOVITZ

Acknowledge**ments**

The Milk Mustache Campaign is funded by the Dairy Industry as part of an effort to increase milk consumption and educate consumers on the benefits of drinking milk.

Specifically, we would like to thank and acknowledge:

The Milk Processor Education Program — Over 400 U.S. milk processors contribute funds to provide national advertising and promotion for milk. Special thanks to Kurt Graetzer, Tom Nagle, Linwood Tipton, Corinne Schwartz, Clay Detlefsen, Sam DiCarlo, Ron Rubin, Wayne Watkinson, Jim O'Hara, Victor Zaborsky, Julie Buric, Susan Ruland, Kikke Riedel, Mandi Bagnal, Rebecca Moser, Amy Heinemann, Ann Ocana, Mark Ezell, Sylvia Oriatti, Rick Beaman, Scottie Mayfield, Dick Robinson, and Scott Charlton.

Dairy Management, Inc. — DMI is the organization responsible for increasing demand for U.S. produced dairy products on behalf of America's dairy farmers. DMI and state and regional organizations manage the programs of the American Dairy Association, the National Dairy Council, and the U.S. Dairy Export Council. Special thanks to Herman Brubaker, Tom Gallagher, Gordon McDonald, Craig Plymesser, Steve Fauntleroy, Madlyn Daley, Mary Pat Anders, Jean Ragalie, Allison Madell, Sherie Gergely, Carol Ostling, Marykate Ginter, Grant Prentice, Julian Toney, Greg Miller, Doug DiRienzo, and Tom Comerlo.

We would also like to thank the following people who have contributed to the completion of this book: Janis Donnaud, Val Strenk, Deborah Stotzky, Anne Schoell, Vickie Rannazzi, Daniella Stollman, Brian Enright, Susan Pecha, Sandy Lieb, Schawk Inc., and BSMG Worldwide. Thanks also to the following people who have contributed to the development of the Milk Mustache ads: Tom Bernardin, Tony Granger, Anthony Arena, Brent Bouchez, Soo Mean Chang, Mark Chmiel, Joan Dufresne, Gary Feldman, Erica Fite, Bruce Frisch, Peter Gardiner, Adam Goldfarb, Kathi Gulotta, Amber Hahn, Katie Herniman, Dave Holloway, Jill Kauffman, Dan Kendall, Lillian Kennedy, Ken Linkletter, David Lloyd, Christine Mammes, Michelle Mascena, Shannon McQuillan, Michell Milano, Tom Millar, David Nobay, Michael Rhome, Rob Rooney, Josh Schildkraut, Alisa Schindler, Ellen Stone, Linda Swanson, Bob Taber, Ethel Uy, Rusty Wakelin, and Holly Zierk. And special thanks to Charles Peebler, Gene Bartley, Jay Schulberg, and Jennifer Mantz.